The Echoes of a Fading Rainbow

Through the lens of a Teenager

Sanya Shah

BookLeaf Publishing

India | USA | UK

To the dreamers, the wanderers, and

those who dare to ask "Why not?",

To the hearts that seek truth in the quiet

and the souls that find beauty in the mess of it all.

This book is for you, for every step forward,

every pause held, and every story left untold.

Acknowledgement

With heartfelt gratitude, I thank the quiet wonders of the world, the rainbows, the rustle of leaves in the breeze, the steady flow of rivers, and the soft embrace of the earth beneath my feet. These moments of simplicity have been my guides, offering both reflection and clarity. They have shaped the words within these pages. Thank you for providing both solace and inspiration.

A special thank you to my readers, whose love for poetry makes this journey worthwhile. Your curiosity to dive into these pages, to engage with the words and the world within them, is the heart of this book.

Preface

At sixteen, the world feels like an endless maze of questions, emotions, and moments that slip through your fingers before you can name them. Writing this collection became my way of holding onto those moments, both the joyful and the heavy, the certain and the unknown.

Each poem in *The Echoes of a Fading Rainbow* is an invitation to pause, to feel, and to discover the beauty of life. This book isn't just about my story, it is about finding your own reflections in the words and making them yours.

Because even when the colors of life seem to fade, a spark always lingers, waiting to reignite the rainbow within you.

TABLE OF CONTENTS

The Joy of Fresh Starts

A blank page, a canvas untouched,
an unexplored galore, a treasure unfurled.
With every word, a new journey begins,
Where none have yet been.
No shadows to tether, no limits to confine,
Just chaos and beauty in perfect design.

A writer, with pen poised, a story to weave,
A fresh start, a new tale, they yearn to
believe.
With characters bright, and words shining
light,
Their fable flows, a heartfelt reprieve.

With each fresh start comes a new beginning,
A chance to rewrite the story of within,
To create a narrative of love and light,
To overcome the darkness and strife.

Picture the ocean, so vast and so wide,
Each wave a reminder of rhythms that aglow,
Just as tides ebb and flow, so too we must
bide,
The courage to rise and let go of our woe.

Each step I take is a step towards growth,
A step towards becoming,
The person who I'm destined to be,
I leave behind the burdens of yesterday
And embrace the freedom of being truly free.

So I raise my face to the sun above
And let its warmth wash over me.
I am filled with a sense of serenity
As I repost in the joy of fresh starts,
internally.

Between the Mirror and Me

The mirror is just there,
silent, like it knows something I don't.
It holds the questions I dare not ask,
and answers that feel out of reach.
The face it shows is mine,
but the eyes seem different, like they are
waiting for a change.
The mirror sees what I conceal,
but it cannot reveal the truths within.
Who is this figure?
This blend of laughter and sorrow crafted
by the clock that bleeds the colours of the
fading yesterday.
Between the mirror and me lies a world,
where reflection meets realisation,
the figure just stares back,
a stranger, yet known.
I search for something more,
a glimpse of who I am or could be.
Between the mirror and me, there is no
judgment.

The reflection does not speak yet it knows
everything I cannot say.
The mirror is just there,
quiet, like it knows something I don't,
unwavering, unmoving, and silent.
Between us there is no voice,
only the quiet truth I must face.
For within me, beyond the external,
burns an everlasting flame,
a spirit that refuses to be dimmed,
a vision that sees beyond the clouds,
a mind that refuses to be boxed in,
a dream that refuses to die.
The space between the mirror and me is not a
void,
but a ground where hope takes root, it is not
a gap
but a moment where the reflection becomes
more than just a face,
where each glance is a step closer to
understanding,
where the past no longer defines,
between the mirror and me.

Maybe God meant Love

As we were watching the stars, the night sky
grew darker.
"Can I tell you a secret?" He asked turning
his gaze towards me.
"Anything," I responded,
Maybe God made the night dark
to show that even in the darkness,
the stars can still shine,
For even when the world feels lost and cold,
light still finds a way to unfold.

Maybe God made animals unable to speak,
To prove that love is shown in actions and
not words.
For in their eyes, in every touch,
Love is felt more deeply than words could
ever clutch.

Maybe God made the moon to remind us
that even miles apart, we're still connected
under the same glow.
The moon whispers softly, "Love reaches
farther than you know."

Maybe God made the ocean vast to prove
that some things, like love are limitless and
beyond our understanding.
The more we try to comprehend it,
the deeper we fall into the ocean's endless
waves.

Maybe God made the earth beneath our feet,
To show that love is the ground where hearts
meet.
Through every step, we find our way,
Rooted in love, come what may.

Maybe God made silence so love could
speak,
In the quiet moments, love feels complete.
For in the stillness, hearts can find,
The deepest truths that words can't bind.

Maybe God meant love,
And yet we're still searching for its meaning.

Lessons from the Heart of the Forest

Oh ancient tree, whose roots delve
far and deep,
What wisdom have you gained,
as the winds start to leap?
You stand so tall, your branches brushing
the endless sky,
What lessons lie within your bark,
as the seasons come and drift by?

I have felt the touch of spring's first kiss
upon my leaves,
And weathered storms that shook my
limbs, though I did not break or grieve.
Through winter's cold breath,
I stood my ground, my will beginning to
shine,
For I have learned, patience grows in life,
with time divine.

But how do you remain so still,
While I, a transient soul, find myself
consumed with frills?
Do you not long to move, to stretch beyond
your place,
To chase the wind,
to feel the sun upon your face?

The wind I feel, it speaks to me even
though I remain in place.
And oh the sun, it paints my leaves with
gold and quiet grace.
My roots run deep, they anchor me, while
branches reach the sky.

In stillness, I find strength and peace,
no need for wings to fly.

But do you not wonder, tree,
What paths emerge as seasons rise?
What lies beyond the forest's edge,
beyond the endless skies?
I try to race against the ticking clock,
in search of dreams to unfold.

Yet here you stand,
still with the wisdom that's pure gold.

I do not chase, for I am where I am meant to
be,
I listen to the wind and let the moments
come to me.
The edge is just a place where horizons meet
the sky,
In stillness, I've found all I need, as time
passes by.

But surely you've felt the loss, as branches
snap and fall,
As storms have torn your bark apart, and
leaves as they sprawl.
How do you rise again,
each dawn,
without a trace of tear,
To stand and face the world brave, year after
year?

Loss is an inevitable part of life, my friend,
a truth I've come to know,
For what is life, if not a cycle, but a river that
continues to flow?
When branches break, new ones will rise,
and roots will find their way.
Through every trial, I learn to grow and
bloom with purpose each new day.

And so you have found your peace, your
place, amidst the turning tides,
While I am lost in transitory dreams,
where endless doubts collide.
Can you share your wisdom here,
beneath the moon's soft glow,
To teach me how to stand my ground, to let
the storm winds go?

The winds will come, they always do.
But you can learn to bend,
To flow with life, to let things go,
and trust that you will mend.

For life is not a race to win, nor something we
can chase,
But it is found in growth and peace, within
our hearts' embrace.

Then I will sit beside you here,
beneath your calming shade,
And listen to the wisdom you have secured,
the price you have paid.
For in your stillness,
I see what I have been blind to know,
That peace is found not in the flight,
but in the Art of Letting Go.

Rest here, my friend, and learn with time, as I
have learned to be,
For wisdom grows not in the chase,
but in the roots that set us free,
In every branch, in every leaf,
There lies a tale concealed.

And in the stillness,
The Universe whispers what the heart has
sealed.

Creating your own Destiny

What if the stars no longer guide?
With no North Star, how shall we abide,
No beacons to light the midnight sky,
No whispers of dreams as the night drifts by.
Yet deep in the darkness,
Lanterns of hope fill the void,
until you rise, fearless and bold,
And carve a path that's all on your own.

It is not a race against time,
a turbulent sprint to the finish line,
but a marathon of self-discovery,
a journey taken internally,
thereupon externally, expanding in all
directions,
embracing the unknown, the uncertain, and
the jarring.

Remember you are the sculptor,
your life being the clay,
moulded by your hands,
shaped by your vision,
sometimes flawed, sometimes imperfect, yet
undeniably yours.
The cracks, the imperfections, the scars,
they tell a story,
an ode to the grit of your own spirit,
a map of your journey,
highlighting the trail you've undertaken,
the battles fought, the victories gained,
and along the way the lessons attained.

In the midst of darkness, a smile blooms,
a deep-rooted satisfaction in knowing that
your destiny,
is not a bound narrative, a script written by
others,
but a story flourishing, chapter by chapter,
with you as the author, the protagonist,
the narrator, the visionary, the lead
in your own orchestra,
a concert of choices, an album of courage.

A life lived authentically, on your own terms,
a life self-authored, self-defined,
self-determined,
where the masterpiece is You.

For life is not a series of laid down cards,
but a deck we shuffle with purpose,
transforming somber fears into golden
laurels,
shaping our realities not through limitations,
but through the audacity of our dreams,
to shape the world around us.

When Fields turn into Concrete

When fields turn to concrete, what do we
leave behind?
The whispers of the wind, the songs of the
pines,
Where once the gentle rustle of golden grains
would sway,
Now echoing silence marks at the end of the
day.

Soft daisies danced freely under the sun's
embrace,
Their laughter now muffled by this
indifferent space.
The fields, once painted with hues of vibrant
green,
Now shackle our dreams in a rigid machine.

The seasons used to ripple with life bursting
bright,
As farmers toiled, planting seeds, with hopes
taking flight.

Their sweat-nourished soil, crafted fruit of
the land,
Yet now, iron giants stand tall where they
used to stand.

The starry night sky, once clear and so bright,
Is hidden by streetlights, obscuring the night.
The cost of convenience, a bitter, harsh price,
The loss of a heritage, a sacrifice.

The children's barefoot freedom, running
through the grain,
Replaced by hurried footsteps on the
pavement, stained.
The scent of sun-warmed grasses, the earth's
rich, earthy smell,
Replaced by exhaust fumes, a suffocating
spell.

The farmer's old plow now lies broken,
forlorn,
The harvest, once plentiful, replaced by the
scorn.

Does progress come softly, with kindhearted
grace,
Or crush down the spirits that once found
their place?

Let us pause for a moment, for there's more
we can do,
To nurture the patchwork of green, to renew.
For life flourishes best in the arms of the
earth,
When we cherish the cycles, remember their
worth.

So come, let us gather, reclaim what is ours,
With hearts set on healing and hands
reaching far.
When fields turn to concrete, let's not say
goodbye,
But forge a new vision, let our spirits fly high.

Wings of Hope

A beacon of light in the darkest night,
Blooming paths with its radiant might.
Courage it gives when the heart feels weak,
Determined it stands, the strength we seek.

Every heart it touches, a spark of fire,
Filling the soul with unquenchable desire.
Guiding lost feet towards their dreams,
Helping them rise against life's extremes.

In times of doubt, it whispers loud,
Just when the heart feels crushed and bowed.
Kindling the will to carry on,
Lifting our spirits till the night is gone.

Moving through valleys, over mountains high,
Nurturing hope that refuses to die.
Opening doors that seem locked tight,
Paving the way with endless light.

Quelling doubts with silent grace,
Reminding us that hope still shows its trace.
Strengthening the weak when they fall apart,
Tending the wounds of a broken heart.

Unfaltering, it stays through every storm,
Victory lies where hope is reborn.
Woven through struggles, it always stands,
Xenial and kind, with open hands.

Yielding to hope, we rise above,
Zeal for life, driven by love.

And in the midst of a gloomy day,
Bridges are built where dreams may stay.
Challenges rise, but so do we,
Determined to climb, just wait and see.

Every single step, no matter how small,
Fuels the strength that conquers it all.
Gratitude flows, as hope fills the air,
Healing the wounds, with love's gentle flare.

Impossibilities turn into might,
Joy emerges out of the deepest plight.
Kindness blooms where hope resides,
Love and light also walk side-by-side.

Moving ahead, fueled by the drive,
Never afraid to dream and strive,
Opening hearts, keeping dreams alive.
Pushing through every moment of doubt,
Quietly, hope shows us what it's about.

Resilient and steady, it never fades,
Strength in hope is what life invades.
Tears may fall, but they wash away,
Uniting the broken, giving them a say.

Visions of beauty in every part,
Where hope lives, there's a healing heart.
Xenial in spirit, a helping hand.

Yielding to hope, we rise above,
Zeal for life, driven by love.

The Pause before the Dive

Beyond the shadow, fear's oppressive hold,
A sunlit meadow, stories yet untold.
A trembling heart, a mind consumed by
dread,
Where courage blossoms, whispered hope is
spread.

The phantom menace, lurking in the night,
Gives way to dawn, and banishes the blight.
For fears a prison, built of doubt and lies,
Where freedom's spirit bravely takes its rise.

A whispered promise, in the darkest hour,
Reveals a pathway, blooming with its power.
It's not the absence of the trembling hand,
But facing darkness, standing firm and
grand.

It's facing demons, in the heart's deep well,
And conquering anxieties, breaking their
cruel spell.

The path unwinds, through valleys dark and
deep,
Where hidden treasures, secrets they will
keep.

But perseverance, with unwavering might,
Unveils the beauty, bathed in golden light.
For beyond the fear, a world of wonder lies,
Reflected in the courage in your eyes.

The weight of worry, slowly starts to fade,
As inner resilience is bravely displayed.
The crippling doubt, that once controlled
your fate,
Is shattered into pieces, by a stronger state.

The bitter sting of sorrow, starts to cease,
Replaced by empathy and inner peace.
For what lies beyond fear, is not an empty
space,
But boundless potential, beauty, and grace.

It's growth and learning, strength that knows
no end,
A spirit soaring, ever to transcend.

The heart that conquers, finds its rightful
place,
A beacon shining, filled with hope and grace.

Through rain and sun, a rainbow gleams,
A bridge between the lost and dreams.
Fear may blind, but light will find,
A truth beyond the veil of mind.

Through storms and shadows, stand firm and
true,
Let courage steer you to skies bright and new,
Sanction courage to be your compass, your
guiding star,
And leave behind the darkness, near and far.

When the World turned Grey

A hue-tiful world, once so bright,
Woke to a shocking, grey light.
The reds, greens, and blues,
Had declared their own views,
And vanished, lost in shadowed cues.

White has gone from the world, it seems,
Lost to the night, erased from dreams.
Yet the swan, in silence, still remains,
A whisper of the light that wanes.

The yellows, so sunny and bold,
Now wither, their warmth turned cold.
Their sunbeams have fled,
Leaving shadows instead.

The pinks, oh so gentle and mild,
Were absent, their presence beguiled.
The roses were pale, their fragrance exiled,
A sorrowful tale of beauty reviled.

The browns, the earthy tones, once rich, now
dull and cold,
Their vibrant hue turns to grayness sold.
The trees, once bold, now weak and slight,
In shadows deep, they lose their light.

The greens, once lush, now lost in air,
The meadows empty, stripped and bare.
No vibrant hue, no life to trace,
A silent world, without a face.

The sky, a dull canvas of grey,
Reflected the feelings that day.
The birds took their flight,
In the ghostly, pale light,
Their melodies fading from sight.

The oceans, once turquoise and blue,
Turned a monotonous, lifeless hue.
A silent, and sorrowful stream,
Where creatures drifted, lost in dream.

The mountains, once capped with fresh
snow,
Lost their brilliance, their vibrant glow.

The winds now howled with a mournful cry,
As shadows stretched beneath a weary sky.

The cities, once bursting with life,
Were shrouded in a colorless strife.
The buildings now decay,
In a desolate way,
The skies were now empty, dull and gray.

A painter, whose palette was bare,
Could only lament and despair.
His brushstrokes all grey,
Echoing the colors that slipped away.

A florist, whose blooms lacked their grace,
Felt sorrow etched upon his face.
His bouquets were pale,
A shadow of the colors they'd once hail.

A child, with his monochrome toys,
Lost the joy of his childhood's bright joys.
His drawings all grey,
A world once vivid, now faded away.

The world, in this monochrome state,
Felt a heavy, oppressive weight.
The absence of hue,
A sorrowful view,
But as night fell, a whisper did start,
A murmur of hope in each heart.
A tiny little spark,
A tiny light in the dark,
A promise of a new world impart.
The strike was now over, it seemed,
A lesson in color, it gleamed.
The world, once so grey,
Became bright as the day.
The value of colour, now known,
Was something beautifully shown.
A world reborn, fresh and new,
A lesson we learned, shining through.
A bright world returned, in view,
The world, painted anew.

Their Silent Grace

In the playground where laughter drifts like
dandelion seeds,
they bounced on clouds of imagination,
pink ribbons dancing in their hair,
a kaleidoscope of innocence wrapped in a
faded dress,
the fabric still gleaming from the day's
adventures.
With a slight tilt of their head and a curious
smile,
they pointed a tiny finger adorned with
bright polish,
the color of sweet cherries,
and proclaimed, "You are very beautiful."

In those simple words, a radiance ignited,
a warmth spreading through my heart,
turning the world's weight into feathers,
a reminder that beauty is not earned,
nor confined in mirrors but indeed
blooms quietly in moments unconcealed.

A group of little girls called me beautiful,
and in their sweet innocence,
I became radiant, vibrant and glowing,
a gentle reminder that alongside the burdens,
lies a beauty overflowing,
in all of us waiting to be seen.
An invitation to appreciate the simple,
to honor the connections that breathe life
into our hearts, that empower our spirits.

What does beauty mean to a little girl's
heart?
Is it found in the glow of a sunset?
Is it the way their laughter fills the air?
Or is it the sparkle in their eyes
when they chase fireflies at twilight?
In their innocence, they simplified
complexities,
taught me beauty is everywhere,
where everyday moments shine like jewels,
and the simplest things hold infinite joy.

Who am I?

I am love,
I am the gravity between the stars,
The hidden force that heals all scars.
I am the essence that hearts pursue,
The quiet strength that pulls them through.

I am happiness,
I am the spark that lights the way,
In the scent of the roses, the sun's golden ray,
I fill the air with warmth and grace,
A gentle smile on every face.

I am strength,
I am the roots that deeply grow,
Anchored firmly where winds may blow.
Steady with vigour, I hold my ground,
In every challenge, my strength can be found.

I am light,
The dawn that breaks the night,
An ember shining, pure and bright,
I fill the world with warmth and grace,
A glow that time cannot erase.

I am voice,
The rhythm of hope that carries through,
A song that rises, breaking through.
A whisper turning into a roar,
Uniting hearts forevermore.

I am free,
A bird that rises with the dawn,
The sky's my canvas, where I am reborn.
I dance with winds, I touch the sea,
Unfettered, wild, and truly free.

I am change,
From seed to bloom, from dusk to light,
I carve new paths in the heart of the night.
With every moment, I shift and glide
Unfurling hopes, a flowing tide.

I am all,
I am the sun that rises, the moon that
eclipses,
The winds that stir, the stars that gleam,
The silent force that shapes the tides,
I am the endless pulse of purest light.

I am the universe,
I am the cosmic dance, the endless flight,
The nebula's glow, the black hole's might,
The whispers of galaxies far and wide,
The timeless rhythm where all truths collide.

I am boundless,
I am the stars that stretch beyond the sky,
I am the rays of sunlight, boundless and spry
I am the heartbeat of the vast unknown
Endlessly growing, yet forever my own.

A Letter to my Future Self

Dear Future Me,

I pen this heartfelt note,
With ink that flows like dreams afloat,
May your days be bright and your heart stay true,
As life unfolds its wonders to you.

I hope you've found joy in the simple days,
In laughter that dances like sunlight's rays,
Have you chased after goals that once made you dream,
Or found peace in moments that softly gleam?

At sixteen, I wonder if you have found your way,
If you are living the dreams we talked about each day.

Are you proud of the steps you have taken so
far,
And growing into who you wished you were?

Do you remember the moments that shaped
your heart?
The friendships you cherished, each delicate
part?
Have you held onto love that once felt so
pure,
And sought out the beauty in what may
endure?

I hope you have traveled to places unknown,
Wandered on shores where the wildflowers
have grown,
Met souls who have inspired you to see the
divine,
In the mundane practices, where spirits
entwine.

I hope you reflect on the roads that you've
crossed,
And treasure the lessons that were never lost,
For life is a journey with paths yet unseen,
And I wish for you, strength to chase every
dream.

Remember to pause, to breathe in the air,
To savor each moment, and feel the flare,
When faced with decisions, let wisdom lead
on,
For tomorrow will dawn, with new hopes to
spawn.

So here's to our dreams, let them soar and
expand,
With hearts full of passion, let's make life
grand.
May your path be bright, with hope as your
guide,
And may love surround you, with arms open
wide.

With love from the past, I send you this plea,
Cherish each moment, let joy set you free.
Embrace all that's ahead with an open heart's
grace,
For the gift of our journey is time's sweet
embrace.

Forever, your past self, with ink on the page,
A light that ignites, no matter the stage.
May the adventures abound, and your heart
always sing,
In the symphony of life, let hope be the
spring.
Just know that there is a past version of you
That is so proud of how far you have come.

With love,
Sanya

The Universe in a Single Blink

In the stillness, the cosmos hums,
Time shifts silently as life becomes.
A spark ignites, then fades away,
Leaving its trace in the fabric of the day.

In the blink of an eye, a star can ignite,
Glowing radiantly, a burst of pure light.
Then vanishes softly, swallowed by night,
Leaving behind only the faintest of sights.

In the blink of an eye, a flower can bloom,
Revealing its petals, escaping the gloom.
Then shrivel and fall, its vibrant hues gone,
A momentary beauty, a life quickly drawn.

In the blink of an eye, a heart can be broken,
Shattered and crumbled, its pulse unspoken.
A tear falls unnoticed, a silent despair,
A scar left unhealed, a load to bear.

In the blink of an eye, a love can begin,
A spark igniting, a passion within.
Two souls intertwining, a destined embrace,
A promise whispered, a smile on each face.

In the blink of an eye, a life can depart,
Leaving behind memories, etched on the
heart.
A final goodbye, a soul taking flight,
Leaving behind shadows, and fading starlight.

In the blink of an eye, a child takes its first
breath,
Entering the world, with wonder and depth.
A tiny heart beats, full of grace,
A new journey begins, in this vast space.

In the blink of an eye, a decision is made,
A path is selected, a choice bravely swayed.
The future is reformed, the course is
redefined,
Though consequences ripple, throughout
space and time.

In the blink of an eye, the truth can be seen,
An epiphany appearing, previously unseen.
Understanding blooms, casting out night,
Guiding our steps towards the light.

In the blink of an eye, the universe expands,
A star fades away, slipping through our hands.
Time moves like light, swift and unknown,
In an instant, the cosmos is luminously
shown.

So cherish each moment, within this brief
span,
For life's fleeting beauty is part of God's plan.
A blink of an eye leaves a permanent trace.
So seize every instant, with passion and
grace,
For in the blink of an eye, time finds its place.

Out of Sync

There was a soul, quiet and alone,
Whose heart held dreams, yet to be known.
In crowded rooms, she would slip from sight,
A shadow in the day, hidden in the light.

She was a circle in a world full of squares,
A line that bends, where no one dares,
She traced the vertices, steady and unknown,
A shape that learns to stand alone.

Their laughter is music, but she heard no
tune,
A ghost beneath the silver moon.
They move in sync, their steps a dance,
While she was lost in a fleeting trance.

She searched for a space, a place to be,
A place where she could be truly free.
But the world spun on, too fast, too loud,
And she stood, unseen, lost in the crowd.

They chase the dawn, she chases the night,
In a world that's too bright, she would lose
her sight.
The spaces they fit, she cannot find,
A drifting thought, a restless mind.

But what if this feeling, this burden, this
weight,
Is just a reflection, a gate to create?
What if these struggles, these battles in sight,
Is the spark that will guide her to the light?

Yet in the stillness, hope took root,
A silent power, strong and astute.
For though she felt lost, alone in the race,
She knew deep within she would find her
place.

Through the gentle winds and quiet skies,
She learned to see with clearer eyes.
The world could be harsh, but still, she would
rise,
Embracing herself beneath the stars' guise.

In time, she bloomed, in colors bold,
A soul once timid, now bright and gold.
A spark in the darkness that longs to ignite,
To claim her own space in the stillness of
night.

Nine steps into the Blue Abyss

The sun, a hazy, watery gleam,
Filtered down, a translucent beam.
My helmet on, the world felt new,
The ocean shimmered in every hue.

At the tender age of nine, I stepped into the
sea,
An undersea walk, where I felt so free.
The world above was far away,
In the ocean's arms, I wished to stay.

A pressure pulsed, a gentle, rhythmic beat,
My ocean walk, a strangely tranquil feat.
Coral castles rose, in hues of pink and gold,
Fish darted past, a story to be told.

Anemones, like flowers of the deep,
Their waving arms, secrets they did keep.
A graceful seahorse, clinging to the reef,
Its elegant form brings endless belief.

A school of silver, flashing in the light,
A fleeting shimmer, banishing the night.
The sandy bottom, soft beneath my feet,
A silent stroll, a journey bittersweet.

A starfish clung, a five-pointed star so bright,
Its gentle grip, a captivating sight.
A curious crab, with sideways, hurried pace,
Observed my passage, from its hiding place.

Each tiny creature, in its watery domain,
A universe of life, a vibrant, endless rain.
A feeling surged, of awe and humble grace,
To walk this realm, this underwater space.

My memory etched, with wonders I had seen,
The ocean's secrets, forever evergreen.
The ocean's magic, a humbling, sacred art,
Forever etched, within my grateful heart.

The ocean stretches, calm and wide,
The waves embrace the morning tide,
The world above, now seems a distant shore,
Longing to return, to explore and adore.

I went through depths where time stood still,
Embracing the ocean, a calm, quiet thrill.
Then back to surface, a slow and steady rise,
To sunlight's warmth, being reflected in my
eyes.

Wandering without a Map

In a world where choices abound,
A student like me finds myself bound,
With a degree yet to land,
And no clear-cut plan,
I search for a path, with no map to steer,
Hoping the future will soon become clear.

A doctor's white coat, a noble pursuit,
But the sight of blood makes me faint, a cold,
clammy fruit.
Accountancy beckons, a life neatly planned,
But numbers and spreadsheets, I fail to
withstand.
A painter I would be, with colors so bold,
But the fear of imperfection leaves me cold.

The barista's laughter, a siren's sweet call,
But the tips are uncertain and the hours too
long.
A chef's culinary magic, a tantalising dream,
But a kitchen's hot chaos, a pressure extreme.

A lawyer's sharp mind, arguments tight,
But the thought of confrontation gives me a
fright.
A scientist's work, to question and test,
But the fear of failure leaves me distressed.

A detective's mind, to solve every clue,
But the darkness of danger, I can't push
through.
A pilot in flight, soaring so high,
But the thought of the heights makes me
want to deny.

So many options, yet none feels quite right,
Lost in the tangle, day fading to night.
The weight of expectations, a burdensome
chain,
The pressure to choose, a relentless refrain.
My friends all are forging their paths bold
and bright,
While I wander aimlessly, lost in the night.

Should I follow my passion, though uncertain
and slight?,
Or pick something stable, and play it all
right?
A question unanswered, a road yet unseen,
A journey uncertain, the future serene?
But who needs the answers to what is yet to
come?
When the future is a garden, and we are seeds
to become.

Through twists and turns, I will make my way,
And each choice will guide me to a brighter
day.
For, in the end, I will come to see,
The future was mine to set free.

The Murder Mystery

In a dim lit room, where shadows dance,
six silent figures took their stance,
each one is a reflection of a haunting truth,
each one is a Murderer of a soul lost in youth.

Fear, a specter draped in gray,
lurks at the corners, beckoning dismay,
it dances in shadows, casting its hold,
stealing the warmth, leaving hearts cold.
"What if I make a mistake?" we ask, in
murmurs so stark,
as the light fades slowly, consumed by the
dark.

Regret is a ghost that carries the weight of
choices once made at the hands of fate.
Each moment a dagger, sharp and precise,
stabbing tenaciously, it offers no dice.
"Can I undo what I've done?", we whisper, as
time slips away,
haunted by choices that led us astray.

Insecurity questions our worth with a smirk
and a smile,
doubt drips like venom, each drop a denial.
"Am I good enough?" our voice implores,
as shadows of self-worth linger at our door.

Perfectionism reigns like an unyielding queen,
demanding the flawless, refusing the seen.
With a gaze fixed on outcomes, it twists and
it turns,
corrupting the joy while the furnace still
burns.
"Why can't I do this perfectly?", it taunts with
disdain,
turning our triumphs into shadows of pain.

Loneliness nestles in corners so deep,
a companion with secrets it strives hard to
keep.

In a room full of voices that flounder and
fade,
It builds up the walls where connections are
laid.

"Am I invisible to others?", we quietly wail,
as solitude enters and friendship pales.

Anger rises like flames in a storm,
A tempest untamed, its fury takes form.
It shatters the silence, igniting the air,
With words that are daggers, too bitter to
bear.
"What's your problem?", we cry with a roar,
As the fire consumes love, leaving only ash on
the floor.

In this labyrinth of feelings, a murderer bides,
With a dagger of time, where darkness
abides.
Each emotion is a mask, wearing grief like a
crown,
in this quiet mystery, where innocence
drowns.

The court has spoken, and justice is clear,
No longer shall shadows instill fear.
These six silent figures must take their leave,
For the soul, once broken, will now retrieve.

The Seventh Pulse

My favourite number, Seven, so grand,
A mystical cipher, across the whole land.
It's an odd prime number, yet so sleek,
Indeed a mathematical peak.

Seven days in a week, a celestial decree,
Seven wonders of the world, for all eyes to
see.
Seven colors so bright,
A rainbow's pure light,
Seven dwarves, in the world of delight.

Seven chakras aligned, a spiritual quest,
Seven wonders, each a marvel to manifest.
Seven continents wide,
Where cultures reside,
Seven seas that stretch, where mysteries rest.
Boundless and deep, their secrets confessed.

Seven stars in the Plough, a celestial display,
Seven notes in a song that will forever play.

A number so deep,
Its secrets to keep,
Seven always makes my heart leap.

It's not merely a digit, a figure, a sign,
It's a concept, a feeling, profoundly divine.
A power, a grace,
Leaving its trace,
My lucky number, forever entwined.
With hopes and dreams, forever aligned.

The Art of Missing Pieces

Life is a puzzle without edges,
pieces scattered across the universe,
each one is a promise, a guiding star
leading me back to wonder,
finding not the missing,
but the magic intertwined in what remains.

I find beauty in the art of missing,
drawing depth from the shadows,
finding solace in the light of remains.
The unfilled places, the gaps in my story,
are invitations to dance with the void,
to embrace the wildness of uncertainty.

What is the heart if not a mosaic,
crafted from shards of lost moments
and stitched with chords of yearning?
Each missing piece is a story untold,
a whisper lost in the clatter of existence,
like a melody played in a minor key.

Here, in this imperfect collage of moments,
every absence is a brushstroke,
every sigh is a quiet pledge,
to love not only what is here
but also what hovers just beyond reach,
to understand that life is not a destination,
but an endless embroidery,
an embrace of the art of missing pieces,
where every absence speaks louder than
words,
and every gap tells a story unspoken.

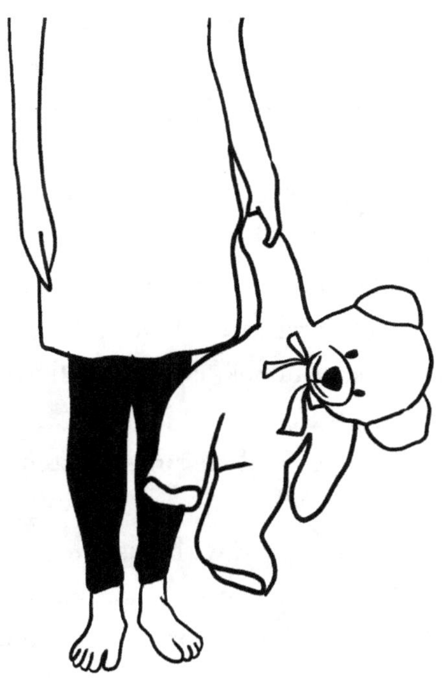

The Memories left in the Attic

The attic air, a breathless, dusty space,
Hangs heavy with the scent of time and lace.
Cobwebs like shrouds drape furniture
adorned,
Where memories gather, tattered and worn.

A chipped paint box, a guitar's case,
Hold dreams long past, a faded grace.
A leather-bound book, its pages yellowed
brown,
Whispers of stories, long since written down.

My doll waits quietly, with dust on her cheek,
Once held with love, now forgotten, so meek.
Her glossy smile holds stories kept hidden,
A silent companion, patiently bidden.

Dust motes dance in sunbeams, slow and frail,
Each one a memory, a whispered tale.
The dust of years, a gentle shroud,
On dreams once vibrant, now a cloud.

In the quiet attic, dreams softly sigh,
lost in the corners where they once could fly.
Faded and forgotten, yet they still roam,
whispering softly, "You can still come back
home."

For though they are hidden, tucked away,
These attic memories, they still hold sway.
A silent echo, a tender plea,
Of what might have been, what used to be.

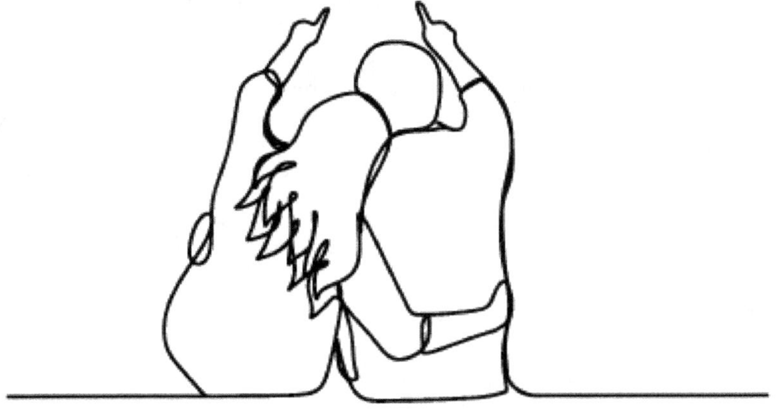

Thoughts of a Comet
before it fades

I am not eternal, only a flash,
Cracking the silence of space,
A trail of preordained whispers,
forgotten by stars.
In this moment, I am alive.
A thousand years condensed into an instant,
The universe watches,
And I too watch,
For I know my end is near.
A scattering into the cold void,
Where no memory survives.
What did I learn on my endless journey?
The pull of gravity like a lover's whisper,
The ache of distance, a silent whimper.
The pressure of stars pressing their
heavy eyes against my skin.
How I longed to be more than just,
a luminous trajectory.
To be something.
I have crossed the edge of silence,
where nothing speaks but light.

My path was written in stardust,
yet all of it was destined to be erased,
But what can I say before I burn out?
What can I leave in this show of light?
Perhaps Nothing. Perhaps Everything.
I will leave with no last words,   but know
this,
I am the passing beauty   of all that slips
away,
the spark that races into eternity,
and in my end, I speak
The language of all things,
That shine,
Then disappear.

Burned too bright to last

There once was a star,
too proud and too bright.
It stood alone, high in the black ocean,
an ignition that refused to burn out.
Others whispered, called it untouchable,
and watched it carve its own path.
It burned without a question, without a
doubt, a force too fierce to falter.
The void stretched wide against its glow,
yet it never looked down.
It burned because it chose to, not because it
had to.
It mocked the stars that flickered below,
calling them mere dust, not worthy to glow.

But, Time did not bow nor did it wait.
The star tried to brighten to silence the end,
but the flame only fed on what had remained.
It swallowed its own weakness, mistook pride
for strength.
The sky no longer whispered, it only watched.

Even the dark knew what came next, yet the
star refused to even ask.
Not even a farewell, not even a sound, just
absence.
What is a kingdom?
When the throne itself turns to dust and
no one is left to remember,
but only the fact that
Even the brightest of stars burn out, when it's
time.

Perfectly Imperfect

In a world full of polished mirrors,
We are the smudges no one sees.
Yet through each blur, we find clarity,
Our imperfections are what set us free.

Perfection is a cage but life was meant to run
wild,
Not bound by the chains of what's perfect or
compiled.
It's the rough edges that make us who we are,
In it, we find the strength to go far.

The moon is fractured and flawed, yet it still
controls the tide.
The sun bleeds across the horizon, yet we call
it a sunrise.
The clouds drift without direction, yet paint
the sky with purpose,
And yet it all belongs exactly as it is.

The world is yours to break and rebuild,
to carve your path, with courage fulfilled.

Through every stumble, rise again,
For in your hands, is the power to sustain.

For when we let go of perfection's heavy
weight,
We discover freedom in being who we are
meant to be, not in some idyllic state.
With every step, with every breath,
A work of art, unfinished, yet
perfectly imperfect in its own right place

So let's toast to the odd and rare,
To the mismatched and the ones unaware,
To the beauty in our chaos and strife,
And the strength we carry throughout life.

And just like that, we are the mosaic of flaws,
Yet somehow we make a masterpiece.

The Contagious Smile

A flicker,
a spark kindling
in the corner of an eye.
Then a twitch,
a slow upward curve
of the lips, barely there,
But then,
it blossoms,
revealing like a flower,
a radiant, gleaming gem.
It spreads,
a gentle plague,
a ripple in the still water of a face.
Across the room,
a mirrored smile begins,
a reluctant echo,
growing bolder,
more certain,
and brighter.
It leaps
from person to person,
a chain reaction of happiness.

A child,
catching the light,
beams back.
An elderly woman,
her eyes crinkling,
returns the warmth.
And even the grumpiest soul
finds the corners of their mouth
lifting, involuntarily.
The weight of the world,
for a moment,
is lifted.
A stranger's smile,
an unexpected gift,
a silent understanding.
A contagious smile,
a tiny act,
a world of difference.
It blossoms,
and it spreads,
and it heals.

And the world,
just for a moment,
feels a little brighter,
a little kinder,
and a little more hopeful.

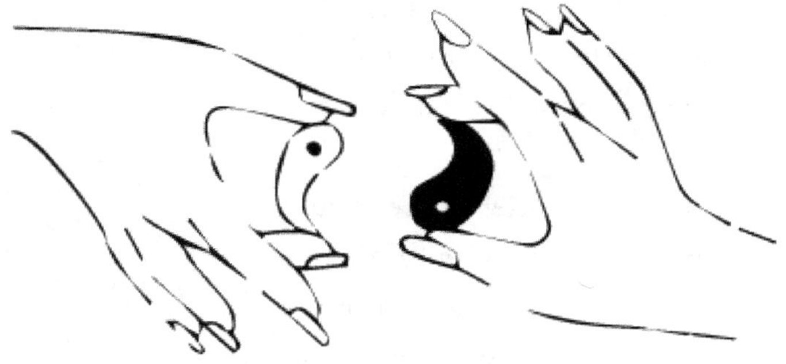

Yin and Yang

The Sun and the Moon, two souls apart,
never meeting, yet always connected at heart.
His laughter, a roaring wildfire,
Hers, a river's soft attire.

He craves the spotlight,
a vibrant flame, burning bright.
She, in the quiet, shines gently,
like the moon's soft lullaby.

He builds castles in the clouds,
ambitious, reaching for the stars.
While she finds comfort in the earth,
grounded deeply, where calmness tars.

Their love, a paradox, a mystery,
evidence of an opposing history.
Two halves of a whole, unique and rare,
a vibrant mural, beyond compare.

They learn, they grow, they adapt and bend,
a declaration of a love that transcends.

Through every trial, they rise and stand,
together, stronger, hand in hand.

The constant push and pull, a dance of will,
a tribute to a love that continues to thrill.
Two souls connected, in a beautiful plight,
a polar opposite love, burning ever so bright.

From Ponytail to Poise

I don't remember when I last spoke to the
person I once was.
She dissolved into time, where waves
caressed,
slipping through the cracks of old routines,
melting into the spaces between faded
dreams.

That little girl grew as seasons changed,
the sky was no longer vast and estranged.
As a teenager, she carried her own light,
never waiting for the stars to shine.

For every bright morning that kissed her
young face,
For nights filled with wonder, for dreams to
embrace,
Not lost, but Grown,
Not gone, but Changed,
a part still present, yet beautifully rearranged.

I carry you within, a part of who I am,
etched in my heartbeat, like roots that
expand.
Through shifting tides and roads unknown,
Your light still guides wherever I have grown.

My hands hold more than what they used to,
Not Things, but Moments
Not Weights, but Meanings.

I do not mourn her, not entirely
Some parts of her were likely to fade.
But sometimes, once in a blue moon,
I almost hear her voice,
soft and familiar,
asking if I miss her too.

I whisper back through time and space,
"I miss you too but don't you see?
Though days have changed and years move
slow,
a part of you still makes me a whole."

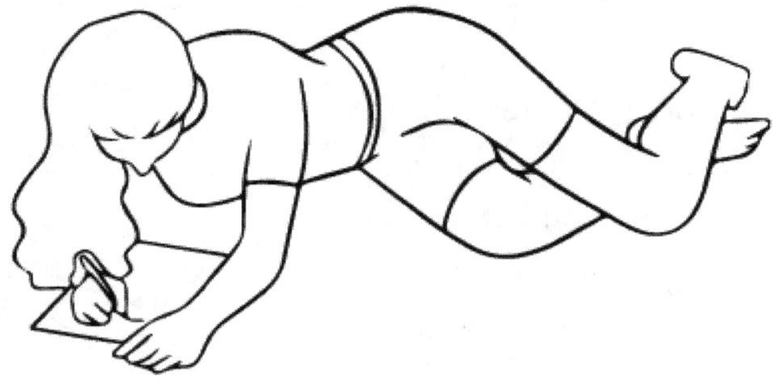

Why the Pen chose Poetry

The first page held hesitation.
letters uneven, ink smudged like,
a voice learning its own weight,
no red marks, no corrections,
just me and my thoughts left to create.

The urge to write pulls me,
like a tide to the shore,
a magnetic pull of inspiration,
a song of the universe,
calling to dance with the stars

A simple phrase, a sudden image,
a flash of insight in the dead of the night.

The world explodes with possibilities,
a universe of words awaits,
waiting to be shaped, to be molded,
to be carved into existence.

To be a poet is not merely a title,
but a longing, a quest,
to find the beauty in the mundane,
to breathe life into words that remain
in the depth of my soul.

Each day, I walk the world,
with ink-stained fingers,
gathering words like flowers,
the soft petals of thoughts showers.

It's a messy business, poetry
full of erasures and crossed-out lines,
crumpled papers scattered on the floor,
a frantic search for the perfect word, for the
perfect rhythm that makes the heart sing.

Yet the struggle is its own reward,
the chase, the constant striving,
for when the words finally align.
When the rhythm finds its cue,
when the meaning shines through,
a sense of completion washes over me,
a feeling of having written something true,
something beautiful, something real.

So let me be a Poet,
an artist with dreams,
for in every verse, every rhyming word,
their lies a universe,
and within that universe,
the pulse of life,
awaiting to be born.

Finding my way in the Rings of Saturn

I am a speck of dust among giants,
a traveller caught in a turbulent spiral,
where paths don't end,
where they only curve back into themselves.

The remnants around me dance,
each a piece of who I was,
but I don't recognize their shape anymore,
they have scattered, shattered and are lost at
the core.

The Saturn's rings murmur riddles,
It's icy edges brushing my thoughts,
and I wonder,
is the way forward or,
just another illusion of space?

I don't know where the rings begin
or where they end,
they stretch out and
a thousand questions spin from dust and
time.

I have lost my way, yet found so much more,
In the eerie moments, I have learned to
explore.
I have questioned the path, the reason, the
why,
only to find the answer lies within my own
sky.

Every coil feels like a mistake,
Each orbit, another question unanswered.
But I must go on, not because I think I know
the way,
but because to stop is to vanish.

I have learned to follow the gravity
that isn't pulling me back,
but forward,
and it is there, somewhere,
in the darkness, that I'll find my light.

The Room I built for Myself

I created a room,
its walls tinted with the variations of my
mind,
a window forever open to the touch of the
light,
where the outside world vanishes out of sight.

In this room, I discover the aspects,
of my own company, the faint changes
in my emotions, the hushed dialogues
with my shadowed self.

This self-made prison,
a cage of my own making,
reflects back a fractured image,
of someone both liberated and bound.

I paint my room with the contrast of my
desires,
but even the colours
cast shadows,
and in those,
the fears, the doubts,
the crazy tick of time,
can be heard and seen.

The door remains locked, but not forever.
every now and then, a crack appears in the
wall,
a beam of light from the world outside,
a reminder that even in my isolation,
I am not truly alone.

That the world, though overwhelming,
is not entirely separate from this room,
this carefully constructed confinement,
that resides, and in its own way,
defines me.
The room, and I, evolve together.

So here I stand,
in the room I built for myself,
welcoming the contradicting,
the sweet and sour pull of being alone,
a balance between my inner world and the
world beyond.

As I slowly unlock the door,
the mystery pours in,
a flood of chaos that transforms who I am,
tearing me apart and rebuilding me,
all at once.

The Art of Letting Go

I used to carry pieces of myself like trophies,
each scar, a story,
each loss, a lesson,
but now I look at what I have held onto,
wondering why I thought it would stay.
Maybe the hardest part of letting go, is
realising that I was never meant to carry it
forever.
I kept everything I was supposed to forget,
thinking if I held it tight enough,
the pieces would stop slipping away.
The trees grow tall,
But their roots are buried deep,
holding onto what they can't see,
I too have held too tightly,
to time, to memories, to voices.
But what if letting go is not forgetting, but
making room for what has been left to arrive?
I stand at the edge of a river,
it's waters whispering its deepest secrets to
me,
that are better lost than kept.

I threw a stone into the stream,
watched it sink without a sound,
the ripples fading,
And I wonder if that's how all things end,
not with a crash but with a surrender,
a fading into nothingness,
like a secret slipping away unnoticed,
leaving only a trace behind.
The leaves fall and I let them,
each one a memory, carried away by the wind,
not emptied,
but freed,
open to the sky,
to the next breath,
and to whatever comes next.
A bird takes flight,
its wings slicing the sky,
with nothing left to hold,
and in that moment,
It feels like the weight of the world lifts,
just enough to breathe,
just enough to let go.
Perhaps the hardest part of letting go is
trusting the space you create.

So I let go,
and watch the pieces scatter like fireflies,
burning bright only left to vanish,
like a snake shedding its own skin,
raw flesh exposed to the world it never knew,
the feeling of agony, freedom, liberation, all at
once,
and for the first time,
I realise I am nothing and everything.
So I let go,
knowing that my Tears are no longer a sign of
weakness but a testament to the courage it
took me to break free.